my first picture dictionary

drawings by Gillian Chapman

TIGER BOOKS INTERNATIONAL
LONDON

Aa

arch

asleep

ant

alphabet

apple

afraid

alligator

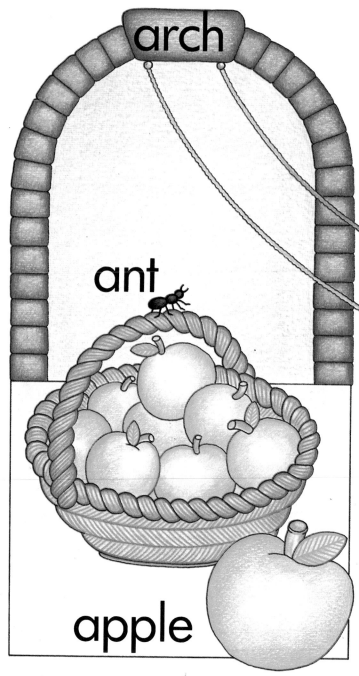

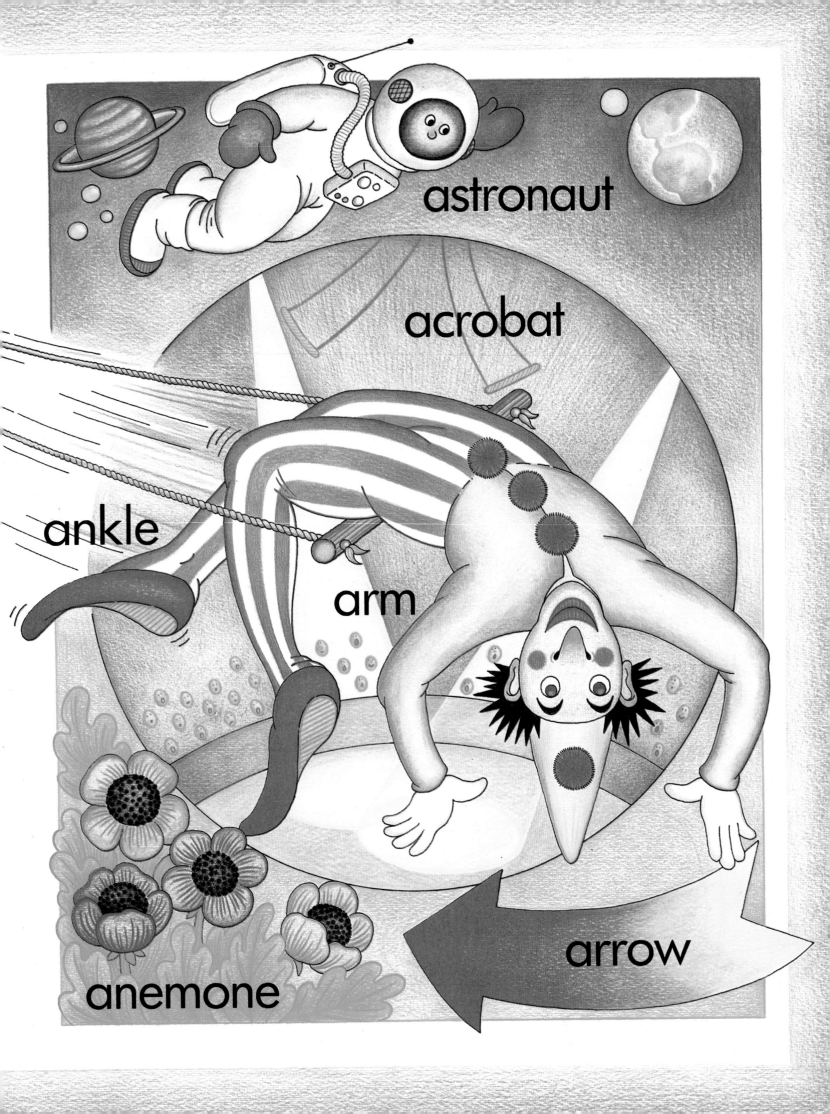

astronaut

acrobat

ankle

arm

arrow

anemone

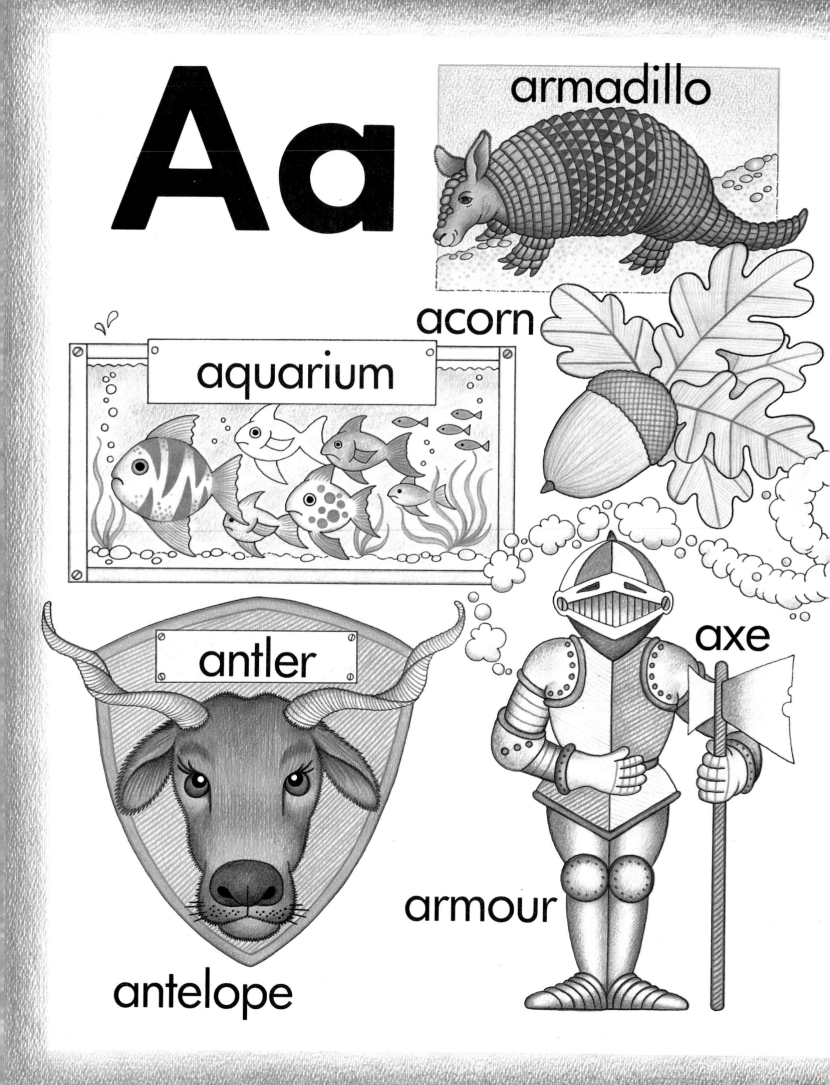

Aa

armadillo

acorn

aquarium

antler

axe

armour

antelope

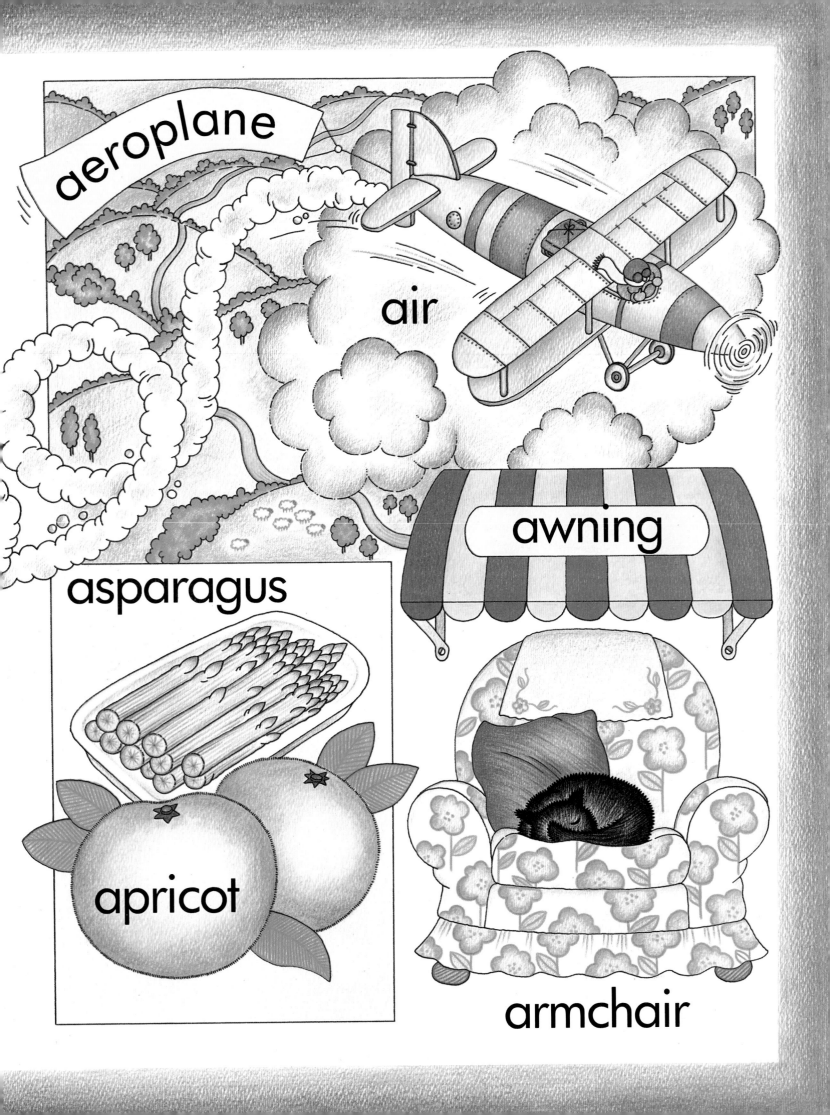

aeroplane

air

awning

asparagus

apricot

armchair

Bb

bald

brush

barrow

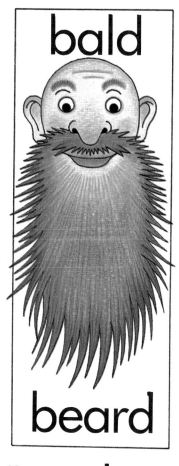

beard

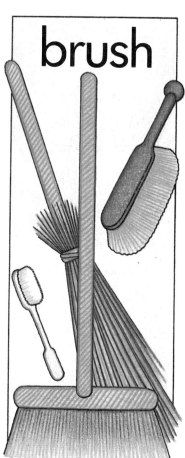

button

belt

burglar

bubbles

bell

bath

bird

butterfly

balloon

bees

beans

box

brown
bear

bun

bananas

basket

bottle

book

bag

bucket

Bb

baby

breakfast

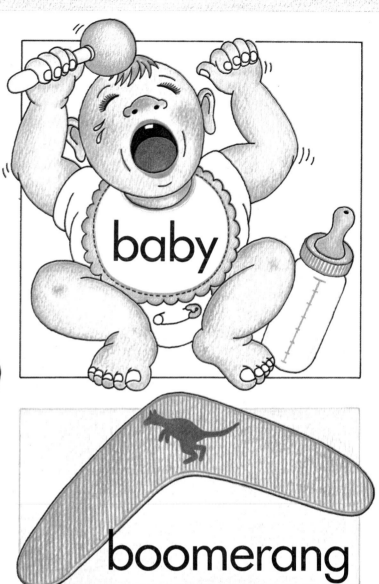

boomerang

bicycle

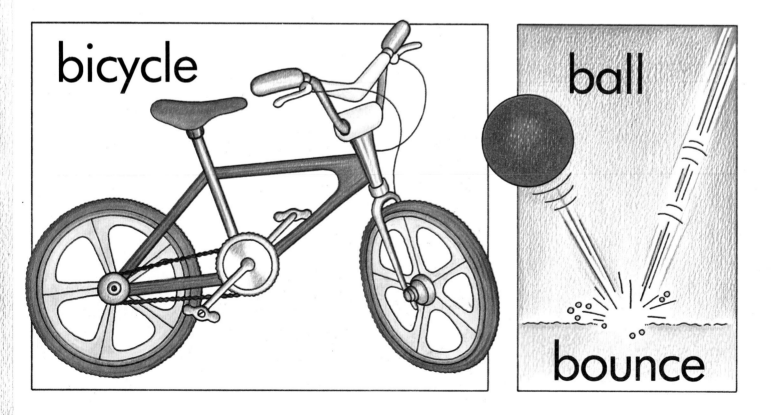

ball

bounce

bull

bush

bandage

blanket

bed

boots

blackberry

badger

beetle

buttercup

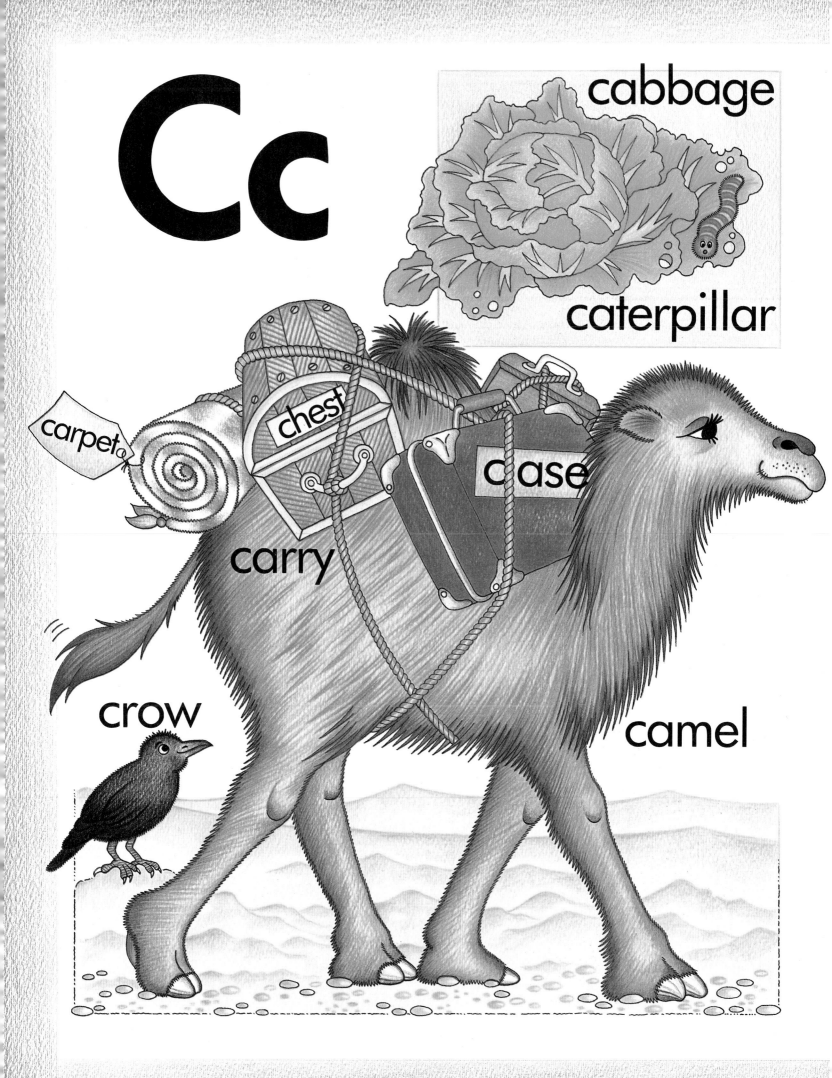

chipmunk

catkins

castle

cannon

canoe

chicken

clothes

cheese

Cc

cage

chimpanzee

chocolate

cold

cat

crab

candle

chain

Dd

drum

daisy

donkey

dirty

dog

dig

draw

drawing

deep

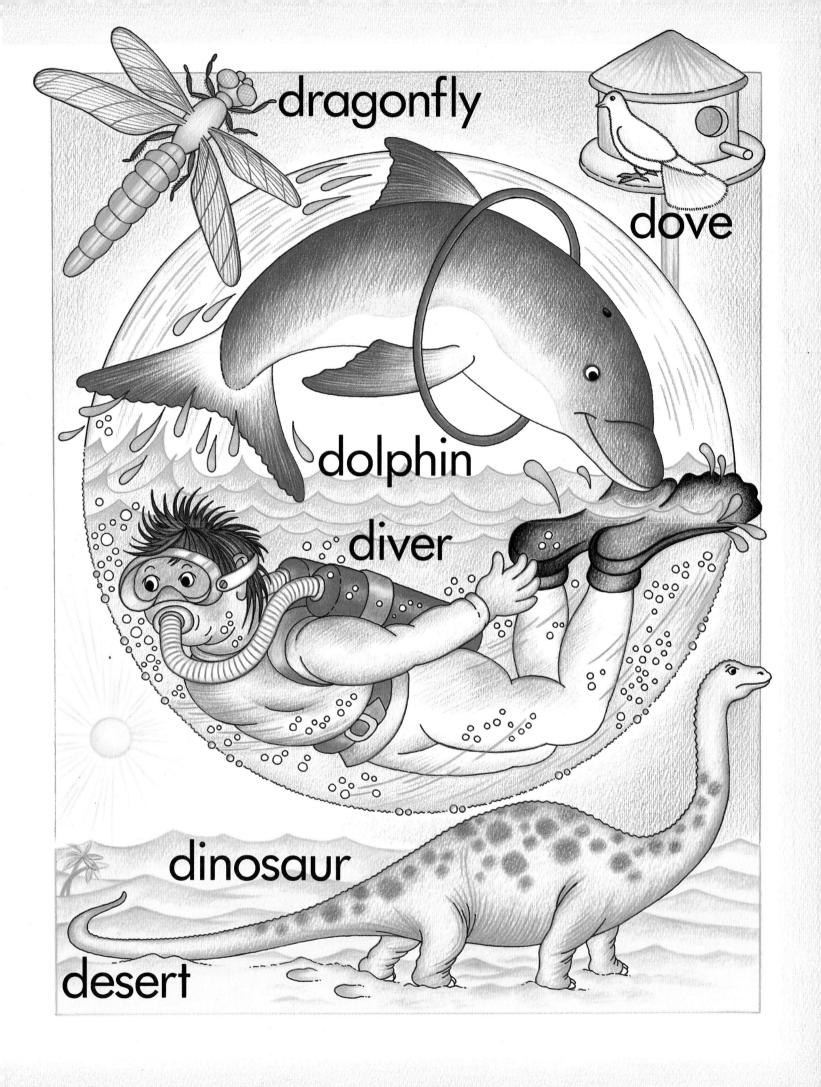

dragonfly

dove

dolphin

diver

dinosaur

desert

Dd

drip

dish

drink

duck

dinner

daffodil

doctor

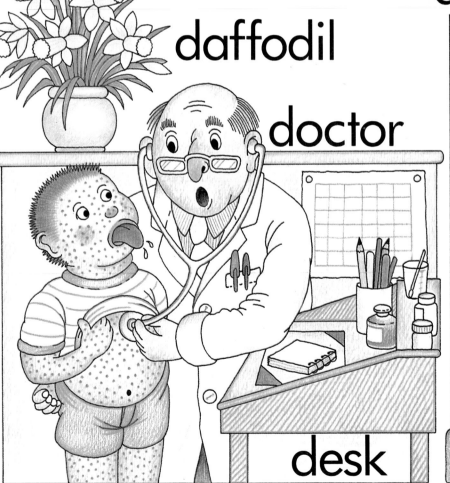

desk

door

dark

dragon

dream

doughnuts

dress

doll

Ee

eagle

easel

eel

eat

elbow

eight eggs

explosion

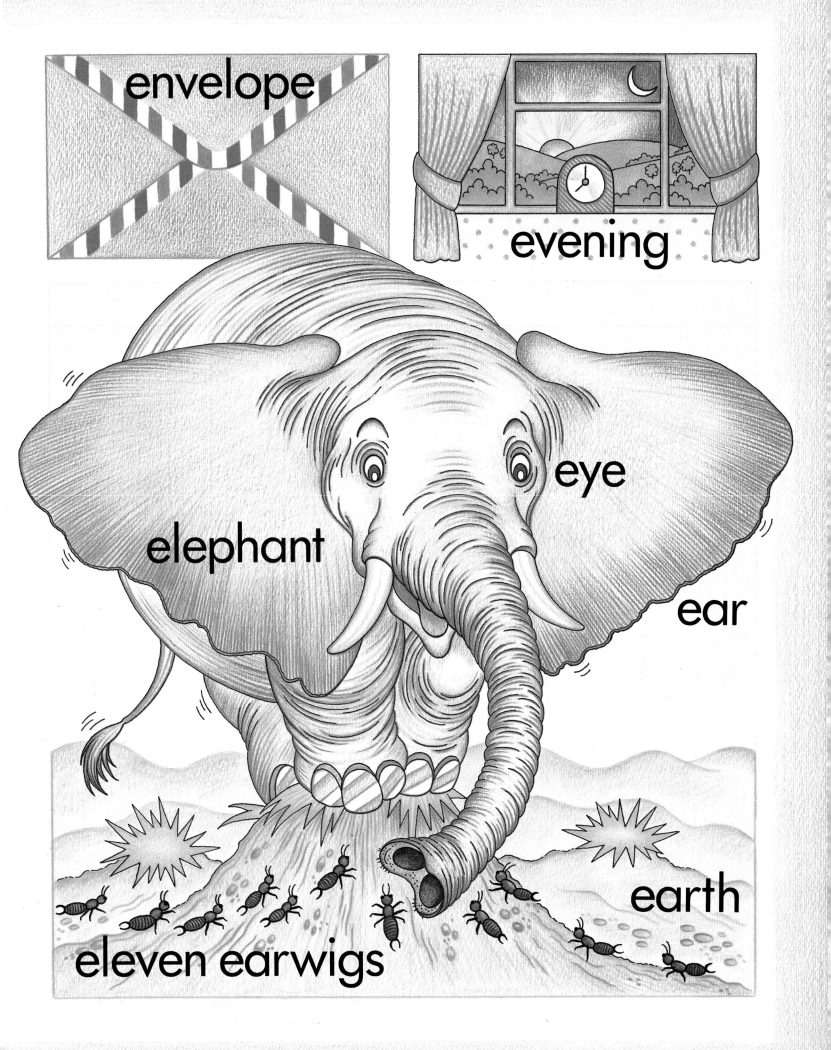

envelope

evening

eye

elephant

ear

earth

eleven earwigs

F f

face

funny

fruit

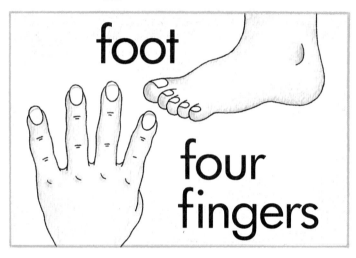

foot

four
fingers

feather

fan

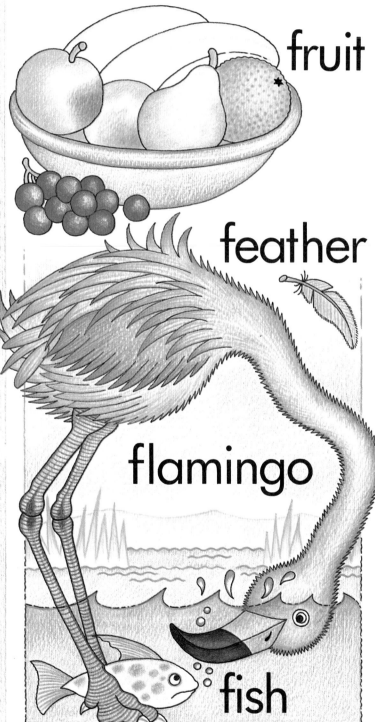

flamingo

fish

flame

fire

flag

five flowers

forest

fir

fox

fence

fungus

fern

fly

fir cone

frog

G g

gingerbread

greedy gorilla

glue

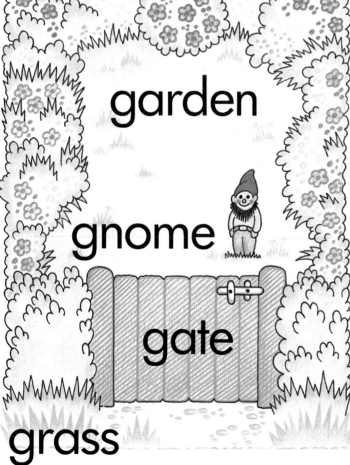

garden

gnome

gate

grass

glass

ghost

gravy

girl

green

gloves

giraffe

grey

goal

Hh

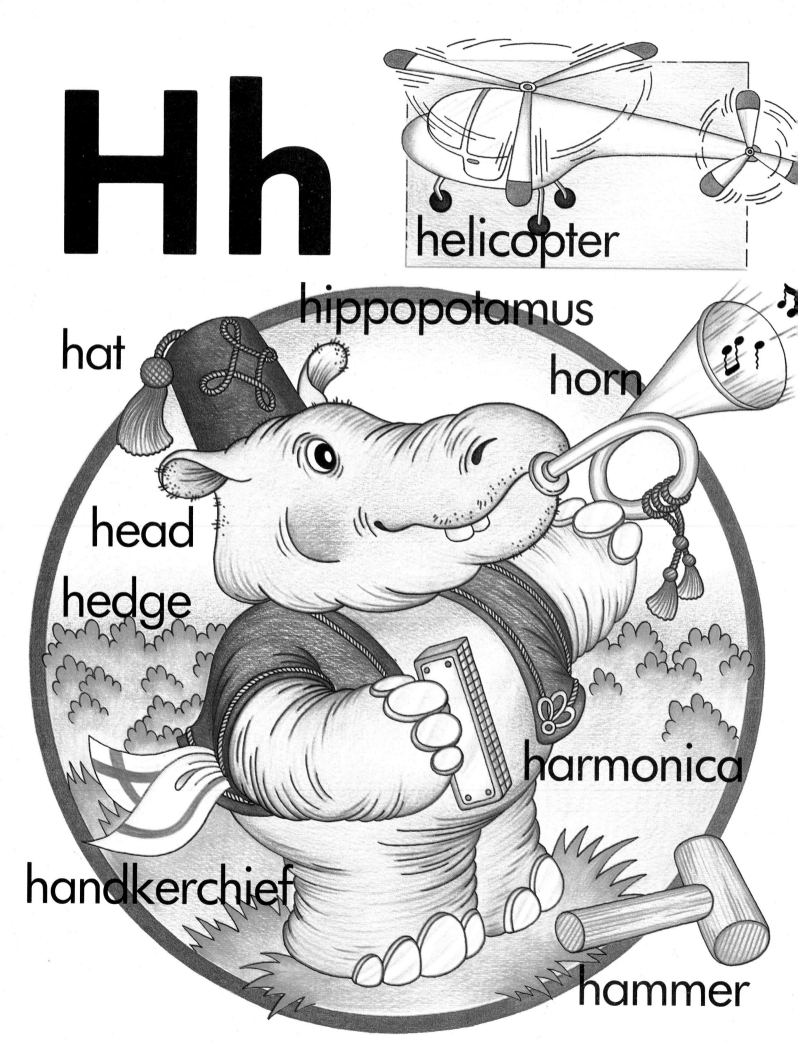

helicopter

hippopotamus

hat

horn

head

hedge

harmonica

handkerchief

hammer

hair

hairdryer

hamper

handle

horse

heart

holly

hedgehog

hay

Hh

hill

house

hive

hut

hold

honey

hoop

hamburger

hop

Ii

icicle

iceberg

ice cream

igloo

ice

island

icing

iron

insect

ink

Jj

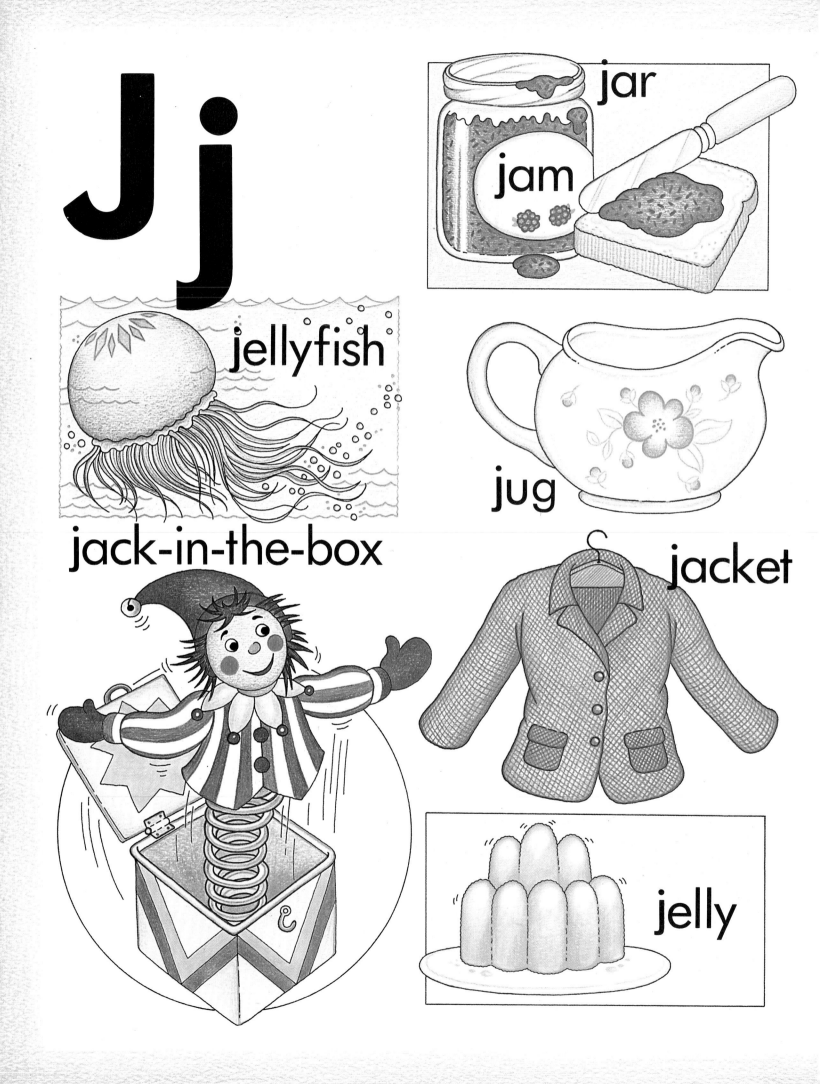

jar

jam

jellyfish

jug

jack-in-the-box

jacket

jelly

juggling

jagged

javelin

jester

jewellery

jump

K k

kookaburra

key

koala

kilt

kangaroo

knee

kennel

kite

knock

knitting

knot

knob

kitten

kitchen

kettle

knife

L l

lamp

light

lightning

leak

lion

leopard

lick

lollipop

leg

log

leaf

lemon

lime

lobster

luggage

label

ladder

M m

mask

mouth

mirror

medicine

map

milkshake

milk

mitten

mole

mud

mop

messy

N n

newt

nib

net

nine

notebook

numbers

needle

napkin

noodles

nose

necklace

neck

newspaper

nest

nail

notice-board

night

night cap

night shirt

nuts

O o

oblong

one **1**

ostrich

oven °

orchid

old over-coat

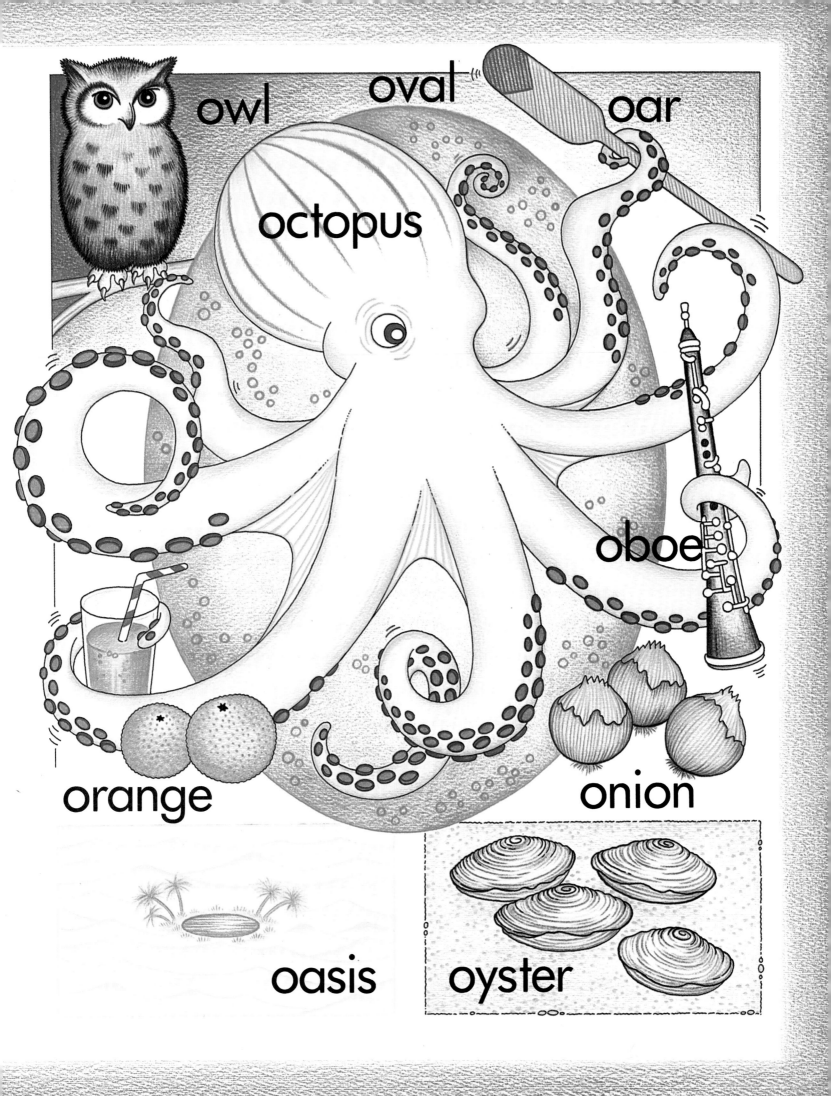

owl

oval

oar

octopus

oboe

orange

onion

oasis

oyster

P p

present

puffin

pirate

pipe

patch

post

pocket

pearls

pie · peas
plate · potato

pond

photograph

pigeon

plum
pear

puppet

pineapple

P p

parrot

palm

point

panda

picture

pig

pencil

pen

pancake

piano

parcel

puppy

painter

path

Q q

$\frac{1}{4}$ quarter

question mark

quince

quiver

quiche

quilt

queen

quill

quail

Rr

rocket

rabbit

rocking-horse

radio

roller-skates

ruler

Recipe

rolling pin

ram

Ss

snake

spider

strawberry

spoon

splash!

sea

snow

snail

snowman

sock

shoe

star

sky

spaceship

S s

stamps

S. Smith
1 South Street

scissors

snowdrops

snip — sew

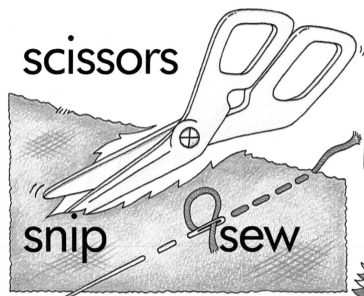

spaghetti

scarf

swan

shadow

swim

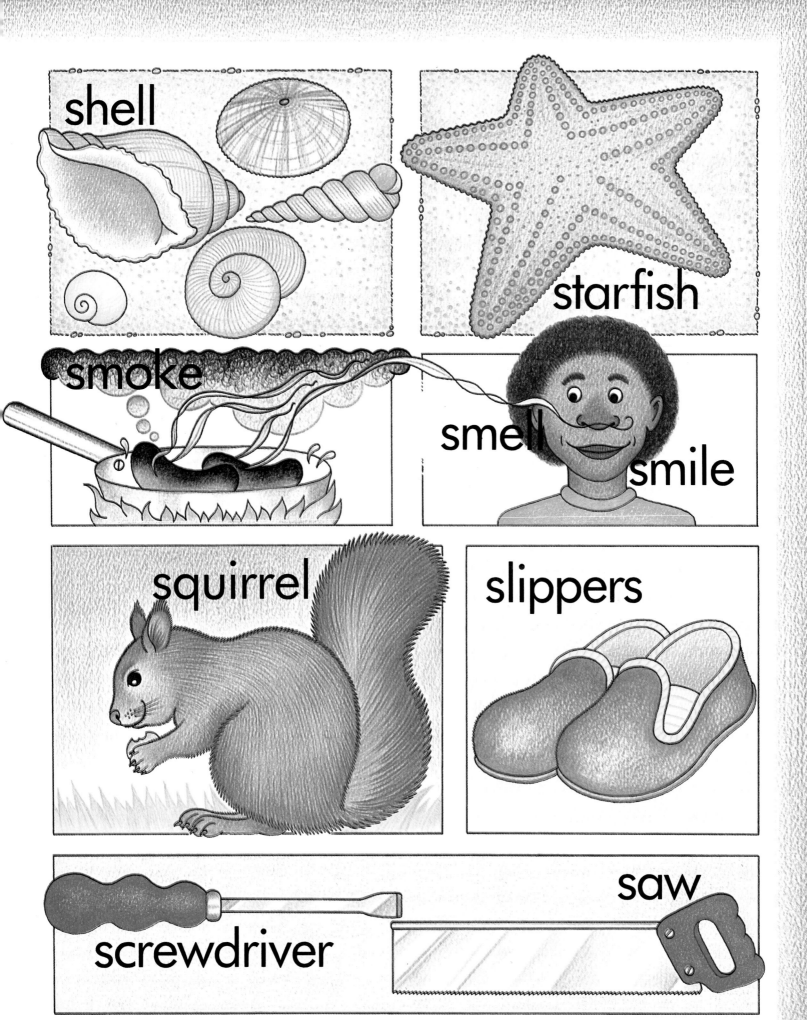

shell

starfish

smoke

smell

smile

squirrel

slippers

screwdriver

saw

T t

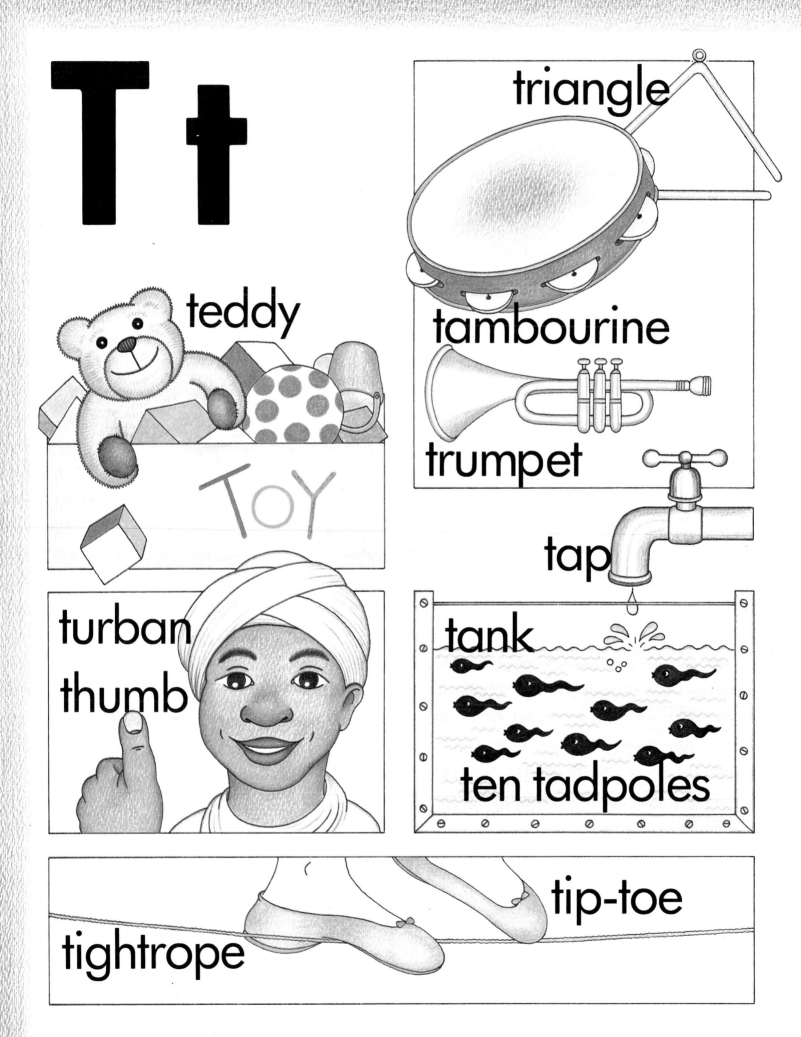

triangle

teddy

tambourine

trumpet

tap

turban
thumb

TOY

tank

ten tadpoles

tip-toe

tightrope

T t

tunnel

ticket

trampoline

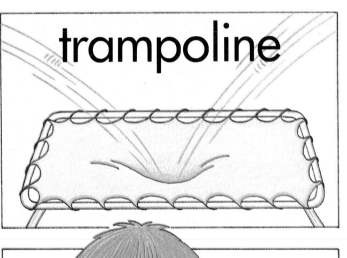

television

teeth

tart

tortoise

thistle

track

train

toad

tie

tower

tallest

taller

tall

tiny

three trees

twig

teepee

U u

umbrella

underwear

unhappy
unicorn

urn

upside
down

Vv

vulture

vegetables

valley

volcano

violin

violets

vase

Ww

washing machine

wool

woodpecker

wasp

window

wristwatch

walrus

whistle

water

wet

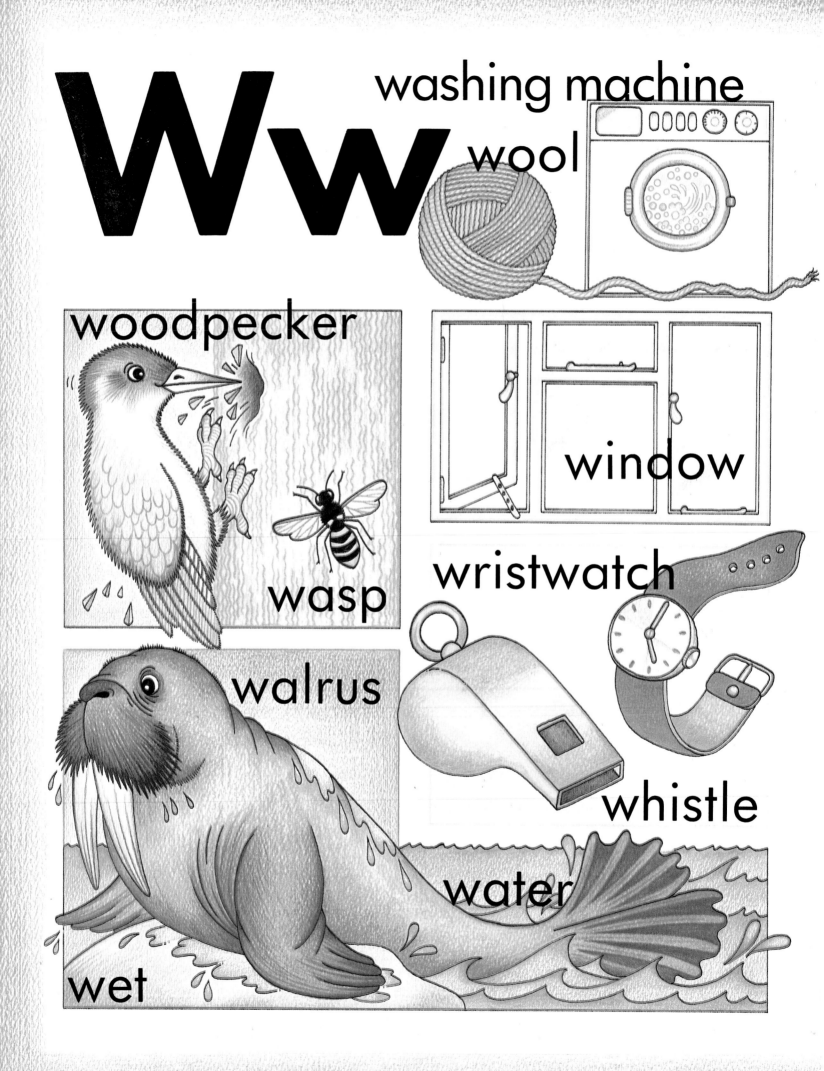

web

wand

witch

windmill

wind

wolf

whiskers

weeds

X Y Z

X-ray

xylophone

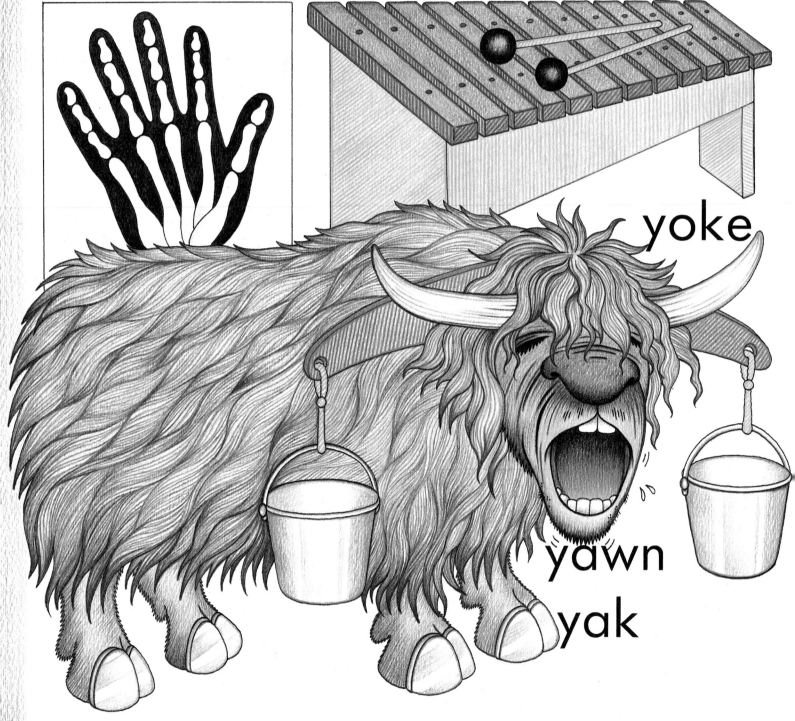

yoke

yawn

yak